The Starter Home*

Volume Two

Positioning

The starter home* project began with a question – how could an architecture office, OJT, and and a developer, Charles Rutledge, not only share expertise and in so doing create a streamlined, vertically integrated design-development system, but more broadly, how could we collectively respond to what we perceive as a gap in the market with a spatial logic – one that would rely not only on an innovative view of land markets, regulatory processes, and capital and equity access, but would take a distinctly opportunistic view of the totality of the design-develop process.

As an architecture office, we aspire to participate in the evolution of the typology, to create housing that not only reflects the present moment, but is also simultaneously prescient and aspirational. To design a domestic environment is to have a thesis about domesticity, and we feel that a domestic argument should reflect not only patterns of every-day use, but the ideological, psychological, socio-economic, political constructions implied thereby.

The work in this series of books represents some of the many and myriad inquiries that our office has undertaken as part of our exploration of the "starter home," and our construction of our own starter home* argument. What began as a conversation has been absorbed into the office milieu as a shared, progressively evolving obsession. The following is by no means meant to be comprehensive, but rather implicative of an ongoing investigation.

Positioning, Volume I

Editors

Rebecca Fitzgerald
Jonathan Tate

Project Team

Robert Baddour
Travis Bost
Rebecca Fitzgerald
Kristian Mizes
Charles Rutledge
Jonathan Tate

Although Volumes I and II are presented sequentially, the process of developing the starter home* investigation and its built manifestation has evolved with purposeful concurrence. Our hope is that the pilot project, 3106 St. Thomas Street, and its attendant analyses – spatial and otherwise – will be read in their totality: as a mutually-informing, mutually-generative whole, certainly greater than the sum of its parts.

It is equally important to see 3106 St. Thomas not as an end product, but as another step along the way; from the moment of its inception, the starter home* project has existed in broader conversation with those investigations – typological, economic, socio-political, urbanistic – that came before, and those that will come after. Further, a new set of sites, no less "test sites" than 3106, are under development: our starter homes* will continue to evolve as well.

The Starter Home*, Vol II.

Distributed by OJT:
www.officejt.com

All attempts have been made
to trace and acknowledge the
sources of images and data.
Regarding any omissions or
errors, interested parties are
requested to contact Office
of Jonathan Tate, c/o Starter
Home*, 1336 Magazine
St. Suite 1, New Orleans,
Louisiana 70130.

Unless specifically
referenced all photographs
and graphic work by
Authors.

James Casabere's "Subdivision with
Spotlight", 1982

Contents

3106 St. Thomas Street

3106 St. Thomas Street

Aerial of the Irish Channel, bounded by
Tchoupitoulas and the Mississippi, 2015

Developing the un-developable

New Orleans' non-conforming lots

In spite of its apparently contradictory typological evolution, starter home development need not focus solely on sparsely populated neighborhoods in metro areas and suburban and exurban large lot subdivision; there is infill potential in neighborhoods with robust services, amenities, and accessibility. Each urban area has its own under-utilized sites of potential energy.

The metro area is an invaluable amenity.

New Orleans' supply of odd lots is robust across neighborhood types, both in close proximity to the city center and in areas further afield. The particular urban condition that exists in New Orleans is one of overlaid grids; for this reason, there are small-scale odd-lot infill opportunities spread throughout the city. In this case, proximity to resources external to the home itself can be emphasized, and house square footage can be restricted according to the argument that an efficient home in a robust network affords residents opportunities not otherwise available.

Transportation, construction, and land costs

Affordability calculations can be deceiving. Land costs fairly predictably decrease the farther the land is from the presumed city center and land costs in turn directly affect the price per square foot of the home, whether or not the ownership model applied gives the homeowner control of just his or her unit or the land beneath the development as

Zoning guidelines – minimum lot dimensions per unit:

Residential Uses: RS 1

Min. lot area per dwelling:	6,700 sf
Min. lot width:	60 ft
Min. lot depth:	100 ft
Max. height:	35 ft
Min. depth of front yard:	Block avg. / 20ft

Residential Uses: RS 1-A

Min. lot area per dwelling:	10,000 sf
Min. lot width:	60 ft
Min. lot depth:	100 ft
Max. height:	35 ft
Min. depth of front yard:	Block avg. / 20ft

Residential Uses: RS 2

Min. lot area per dwelling:	5,000 sf
Min. lot width:	50 ft
Min. lot depth:	90 ft
Max. height:	35 ft
Min. depth of front yard:	Block avg. / 20ft

well. Transportation costs equally predictably increase the farther from the center you are, and can be a major factor in the affordability over time of a home.

Defining the center

Residential Uses: RD 1

Min. lot area per dwelling:	5,000 sf
Min. lot width:	50 ft
Min. lot depth:	90 ft
Max. height:	35 ft
Min. depth of front yard:	Block avg. / 20ft

For many metro areas in the United States, the ideal of the urban core and the periphery has dissolved, and in many cases the multi-nodal metro area has since inception been a more accurate description of type. Here, the center is marked at the Central Business District in order to illustrate the radial relationship of New Orleans' neighborhoods to the historic city center.

Strength in numbers

Residential Uses: RD 2

Min. lot area per dwelling:	4,400 sf
Min. lot width:	40 ft
Min. lot depth:	90 ft
Max. height:	40 ft
Min. depth of front yard:	Block avg. / 20ft

An "economy of scale" is central to the 20th century ideal of the developer's planned residential community, the catalog home, and the prefabrication process in the building industry – three expressions of the starter home type; for the New Orleans odd lot strategy, the lost efficiency in developing across dispersed non-conforming lots is made up through the application of a responsive economy of scale: each Starter Home* represents its own individual costs, but also its own force within the larger system of Starter Homes* in the city. The variability of property values across the metro area is used as an advantage, as properties function financially in a compensatory relationship with one another.

Residential Uses: RD 3, 4

Min. lot area per dwelling:	3,600 sf
Min. lot width:	30 ft
Min. lot depth:	90 ft
Max. height:	40 ft
Min. depth of front yard:	Block avg. / 20ft

Lot size and distribution

Lot Size

	9,000 + sf
	7,000 - 9,000 sf
	6,000 - 7,000 sf
	5,000 - 6,000 sf
	4,400 - 5,200 sf
	3,700 - 4,400 sf
	3,300 - 3,700 sf
	< 3,000 sf

Non-conforming lots abound.

Odd lots can be found in some of New Orleans' most well-populated, desirable neighborhoods – places where schools, transportation and food networks, businesses and parks are prevalent.

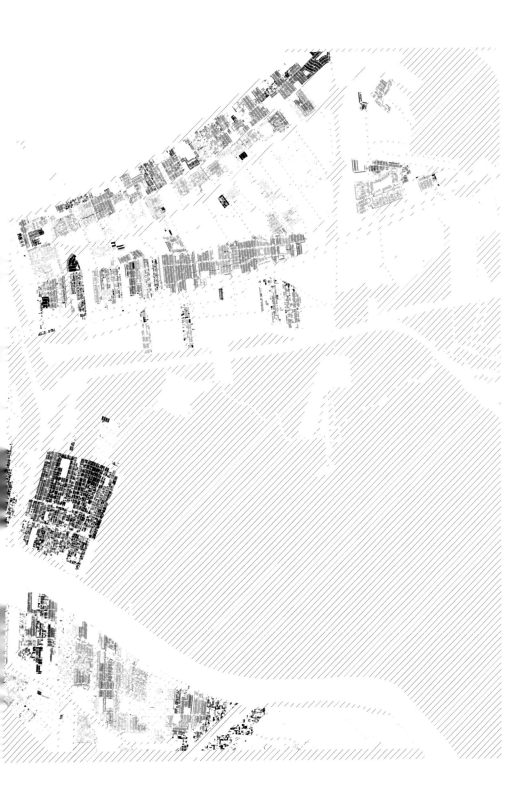

Here are all 5,453 Starter Home* – odd – lots in New Orleans.

Zoning and the city

Zoning

░	HMT: Historic
▦	RM: Multi-Family
▧	RD: Two Family
■	MU: Mixed Use
▥	RS: Single Family

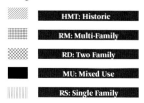

This illustration isolates the Starter Home* lot in its urban context in order to show both the distribution of lots across neighborhood types in New Orleans, and to begin to define the urban strategy.

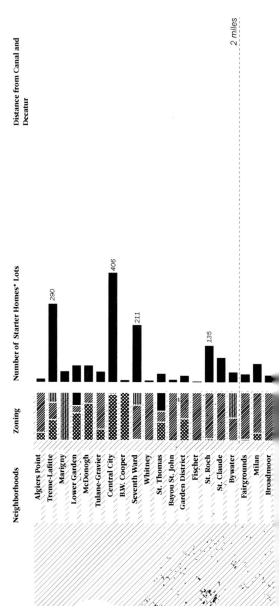

Distance from Canal and Decatur

2 miles

Number of Starter Homes* Lots

| 290 | 406 | 211 | 135 |

Zoning

Neighborhoods

Algiers Point
Treme-Lafitte
Marigny
Lower Garden
McDonogh
Tulane-Gravier
Central City
B.W. Cooper
Seventh Ward
Whitney
St. Thomas
Bayou St. John
Garden District
Fischer
St. Roch
St. Claude
Bywater
Fairgrounds
Milan
Broadmoor

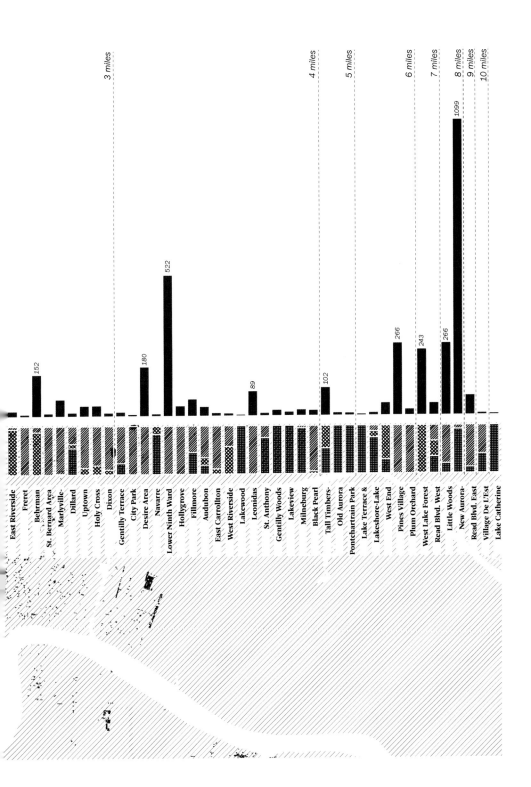

A taxonometric view of New Orleans' non-conforming, or odd, lots is a study in diversity:

leftovers of the land division process, they are ignored by recognized development models because of their idiosyncrasy. Developing odd lots can prove difficult without employing a tactical position: seeing each lot as a potential member of a dispersed, networked urban and financial whole: they require adaptability to catalyze their full potential.

An infill strategy that is both highly sensitive to site conditions and reliant on robust neighborhood resources in fact requires the odd lot as site precisely for the fact that it is undervalued and according to ideal models, considered un-developable.

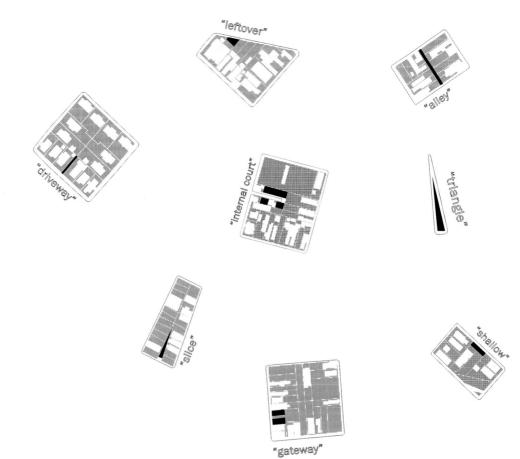

It is for this reason that odd lots remain in otherwise densely populated, amenity rich neighborhoods. These neighborhoods play an essential role: the Starter Home* can occupy the odd lot, placing itself within a network of resources, embracing the constraints of the sites themselves, and remain small, efficient, and affordable.

For our purposes, a non-conforming lot is a lot that does not abide by the minimum requirements set out in the city's zoning code. A Starter Home* lot is, moreover, a non-conforming lot that is zoned for residential use, and does not have an existing structure on it.

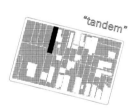

They come in all shapes and sizes.

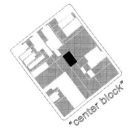

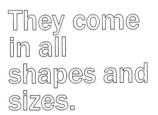

Starter Home*
odd lots, zoning,
and site-specific
development.

Working with non-conforming lots requires flexibility, both in design and in development strategy. Responding to the neighborhood-dependent, site-specific resources and networks available is crucial if the model is to succeed – lot size & shape, proximity of one odd lot to another and to resources, zoning, availability, comparable price per square foot costs in the area are all analyzed according to their compensatory potential with respect to individual lot, to "cluster," to neighborhood, and to city.

IRISH CH.

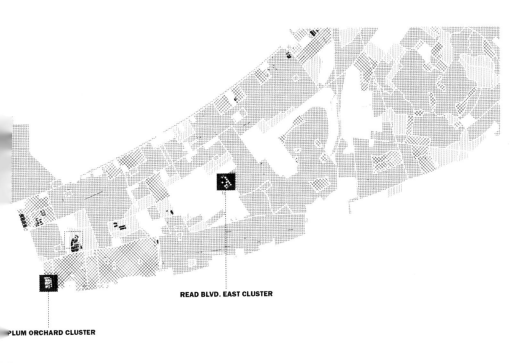

READ BLVD. EAST CLUSTER

PLUM ORCHARD CLUSTER

FLORIDA-DESIRE CLUSTER

Zoning

	HMT: Historic
	RM: Multi-Family
	RD: Two Family
	MU: Mixed Use
	RS: Single Family

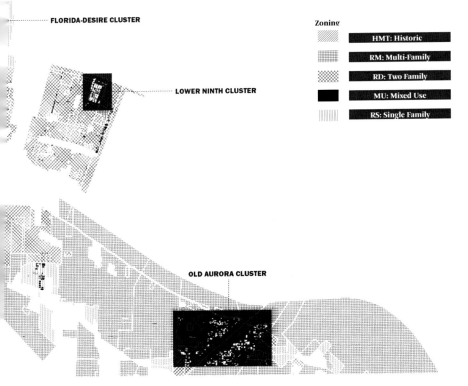

LOWER NINTH CLUSTER

OLD AURORA CLUSTER

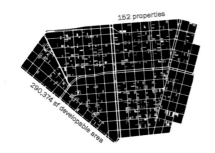

152 properties

290,374 sf developable area

Marigny-St. Roch

Odd Lot Neighborhoods

Odd lots are scattered across New Orleans neighborhoods, from the most densely populated to those with significant recent disinvestment and resulting high vacancy rates. At the neighborhood scale, the Starter Home* strategy adapts to the particularities of place, while maintaining an ideological, economic, and functional relationship to one another.

The following neighborhoods have been chosen both for their individuality of character as well as for their similar status as densely populated and amenity rich; as Starter Home* neighborhoods, they exemplify the possibilities embedded in exploiting existing and location-specific under-utilized land in order to place first-time home owners in areas that they would not otherwise be able to afford.

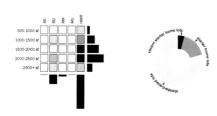

23 properties, 43,830 sf of developable area

Bywater

The Starter Home* can adapt.

Certainly, one of the main tenets of Euclidian zoning is that property values are maintained through single-use neighborhoods and the regulatory barometer that requires developers

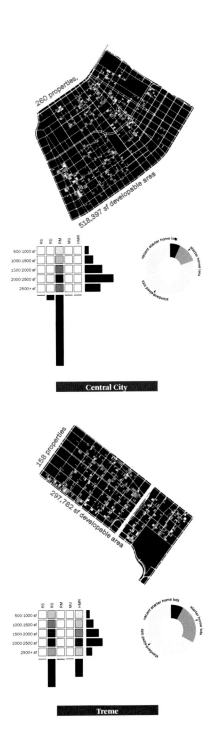

to build at scale with the rest of the houses
in the area. The Starter Home* strategy
questions this long-held standard of the
American planning process, maintaining
that diverse neighborhoods and access to the
opportunities afforded by becoming a part of
the equity market can and should be built in
to any urban planning process.
A development strategy that requires
elements – land costs, development size
and scope, construction costs – to remain
constant is both impractical in metro contexts
and untenable if the opportunities afforded
by metro occupation are to be accessed.
Embracing fluidity in the development
paradigm requires that design be integrated
into all aspects of the process: in this sense,
we respond to the history of the development
process in a way that is not antagonistic,
but rather evolutionary, respecting the
sophistication that has come from a century
of refinement of the model.

The breadth of options in the starter home
spectrum, all beholden to and born from
market forces, can be selected for their
neighborhood and site-specific viability, and
when combined with a tactical architectural
strategy that remains the driving conceptual
constant in the system, function as a whole
much greater than the sum of its parts.

Starter Homes* work together.

The Starter Home* strategy adapts across delivery methods and ownership models. Embracing the spectrum of opportunities that exists within the development sphere can reinforce connectivity, urban exchange, and capital distribution as we engage new models for entry into the equity market.

This graphic illustrates some of the potentials in the Irish Channel, and begins to propose an architectural logic that will be developed on a site-by-site basis.

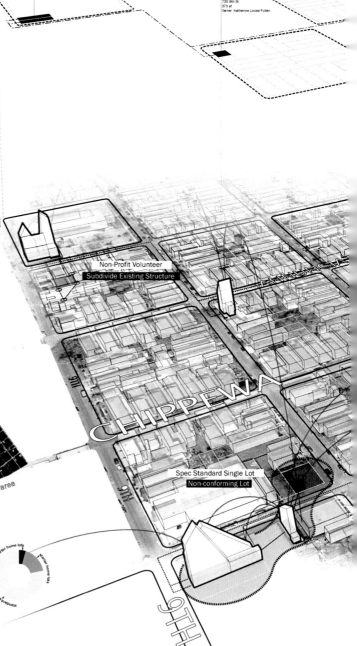

901 & 905 9th St
770 sf & 792 sf
Owner: Orleans Parish School Board

RD-2
735 8th St
370 sf
Owner: Katherine Louise Pullen

Non-Profit Volunteer
Subdivide Existing Structure

CHIPPEWA

Spec Standard Single Lot
Non-conforming Lot

82 properties

149,894 sf developable area

	RS	RD	RM	MU	HMR
500-1000 sf					
1000-1500 sf					
1500-2000 sf					
2000-2500 sf					
2500+ sf					

Irish Channel

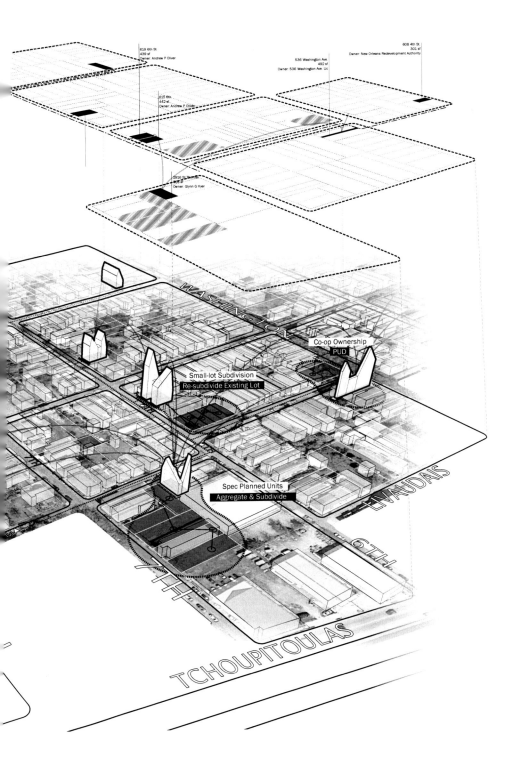

This process exists in the real world.

As much as "The Starter Home*" exists as an investigation, it is also an ongoing process of land acquisition that is by no means direct or simple; many lots as have been identified through the abstract process of data analysis, but relatively few are actually available in any real sense – for a lot type that has historically been undervalued and as a result is often used in ad-hoc ways, finding interested or available owners and achieving clear title are two major impediments to purchasing and developing.

After four months, we successfully purchased one non-conforming lot, at 3106 St. Thomas Street...

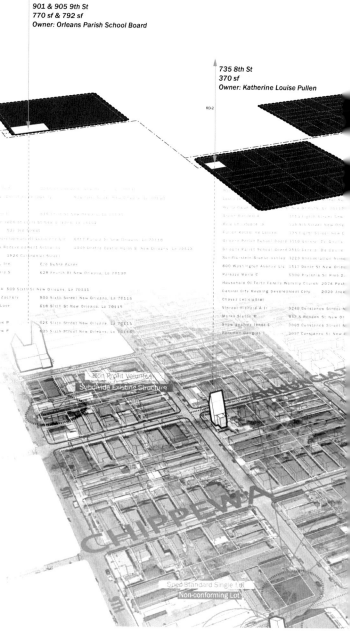

901 & 905 9th St
770 sf & 792 sf
Owner: Orleans Parish School Board

735 8th St
370 sf
Owner: Katherine Louise Pullen

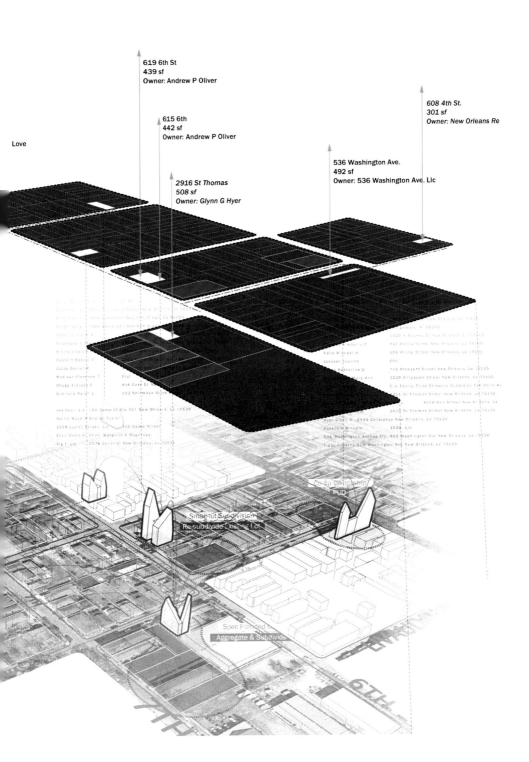

619 6th St
439 sf
Owner: Andrew P Oliver

615 6th
442 sf
Owner: Andrew P Oliver

2916 St Thomas
508 sf
Owner: Glynn G Hyer

608 4th St.
301 sf
Owner: New Orleans Re

536 Washington Ave.
492 sf
Owner: 536 Washington Ave. Llc

Love

The site is all at once a legal definition, an embedded history, a record of activity, and a physical entity.

A Starter Home* expects no tabula rasa, and in fact relies on the specificities of site in order to function at its best, financially, urbanistically, and spatially. The overlay of zoning – both impediment and opportunity – guides the design process but also provides the potentiality of the site as Starter Home* opportunity. Standard zoning regulations prefer standard architectural expressions; the Starter Home* is free to exploit the eccentricities of its particular site, allowing restrictions to become prospects, and privileging the particular over the generic.

3106 St. Thomas

Spec Standard Single Lot
Non-conforming Lot

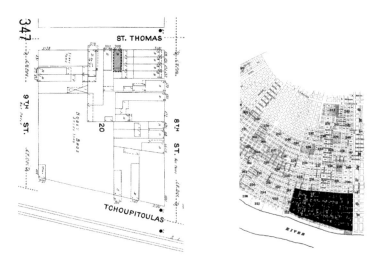

Irish Channel

EXHIBIT A

A CERTAIN LOT OF GROUND, together with all the buildings and improvements thereon, and all the rights, ways, privileges, servitudes, appurtenances and advantages thereunto belonging or in anywise appertaining, situated in the Fourth District of New Orleans, in Square No. 20 (Old Square 8), which square is bounded by St. Thomas, Eighth, Ninth and Tchoupitoulas Streets. Said lot is designated by the Letter "B" on a sketch of survey made by Gilbert, Kelly & Couturie, Inc., Surveyors, dated February 15,1971, a print of which is annexed to and made part of an act passed before M.L. Dresner, Notary Public, dated February 17,1971, and according to said sketch of survey, said lot begins at a distance of eighty-three feet, seven inches (83'7") from the corner of St. Thomas and Eighth Streets and measures thence on a line toward Ninth Street, sixteen feet, five inches (16'5") front on St. Thomas Street, the same width in the rear, by a depth of fifty-five feet, five inches, two lines (55'5"5''') between equal and parallel lines. Said Lot "B" is composed of the rear of original Lots 10 and 11.

All as more fully shown on a plot of survey by Gilbert, Kelly & Couturie, Inc., Surveyors, dated June 9, 1983, a certified copy of which is annexed to an act passed before Frank P. Battard, Notary Public, dated June 16, 1983.

The improvements thereon bear the Municipal No. 3106 St. Thomas Street, New Orleans, Louisiana, 70115.

Form is local.

The advantages of site

Context

Our context is not only spatial, architectural, and social, but political and regulatory:

The Irish Channel is a historic district, protected by New Orleans' Historic District Landmarks Commission – an entity that requires an architectural committee design review before permitting new construction.

The New Orleans HDLC says of new construction:

"Prior to undertaking a new construction or addition project, the HDLC encourages property owners to develop an appreciation of the unique architectural character of New Orleans and its neighborhoods and allow that understanding to inform their design. The HDLC does not require that historic properties be "copied" in new construction, but encourages that new construction be examples of high-quality design and sympathetic to its distinctive surroundings."

Constructing a logic

Massing

Massing exercises began where our a-frame investigations left off – with the idea that the clarity of a diagram could be generative of the first stage of our evolutionary logic for the starter homes*.

Balancing spatial variety with programmatic flexibility is key to the future viability of the overall starter home* strategy: cost mitigation is based not only in rethinking the relationship between developer and designer, the relationship between urban and domestic resources, and land value, but also in time management – the designer is essential, but each design must exist in an evolutionary logic with the ones that came before. Each time a new site is developed, we begin where we left off with the site before – constantly adapting, absorbing the knowledge gained from new investigations.

Looking forward

As more sites are developed, the specific character of each site will become operations that morph our diagrammatic architecture as the system "learns" via the expressions of an iterative design process.

Programmatic flexibility

St. Thomas Street

9TH STREET

8TH STREET

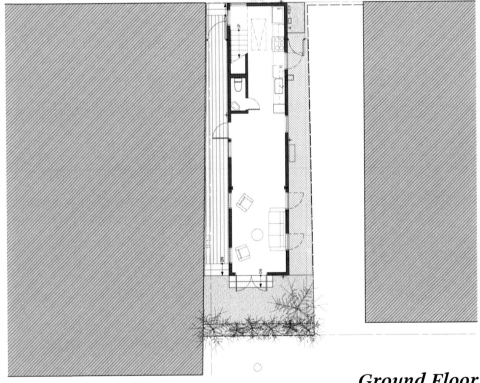

Ground Floor

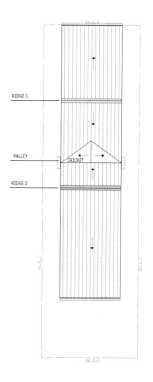

Second Floor   ## Loft   ## Roof

Program

In the case of 3106 St. Thomas Street, the longitudinal section becomes especially important: creating spatial diversity, fulfilling programmatic desires, and establishing flexibility, all while embracing a restricted footprint placed the section at the forefront of the design.

This is not a tiny house.

In order to prove the potential of the model, we sought to avoid the small-lot, tiny-house paradigm that so often dominates conversations about cost and energy savings in the single-family-home market; at 916 sf (net), 3106 is relatively small when compared to the average single-family home, but it certainly is not tiny Balancing the cost-savings associated with lower per-squre-foot land and construction costs with a desire to fulfil programmatic needs while avoiding prescriptive domestic design guides this and future starter home* designs.

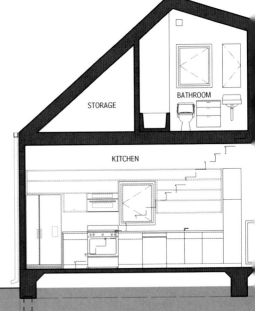

ST. THOMAS STREET

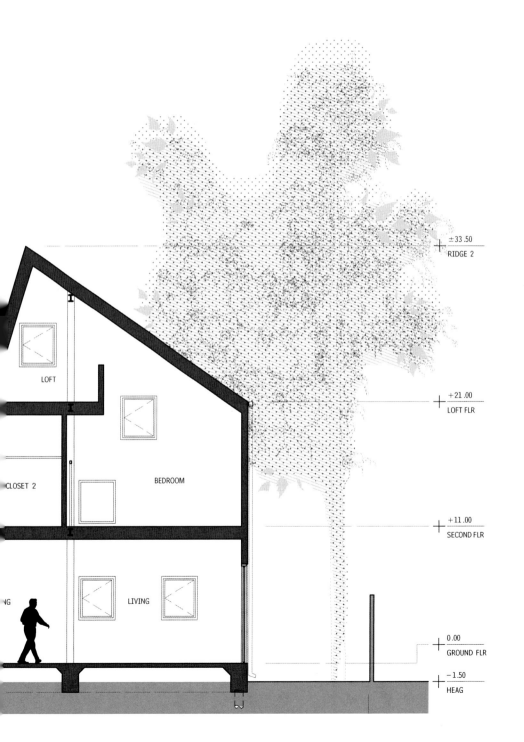

LOFT

CLOSET 2

BEDROOM

LIVING

NG

+33.50
RIDGE 2

+21.00
LOFT FLR

+11.00
SECOND FLR

0.00
GROUND FLR

−1.50
HEAG

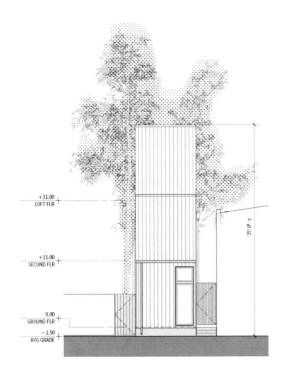

+21.00
LOFT FLR

35'-0" ±

+11.00
SECOND FLR

0.00
GROUND FLR

− 1.50
AVG GRADE

Building the pilot

Meanwhile, we've bought and re-sold properties, pursued lots and been turned away, and arrived at two new sites: 3609-3613 S. Saratoga Avenue.

New sites come with new drivers; a blighted and irreparably destitute existing structure had to be demolished, and we were prompted to investigate subdivision at the scale of two adjoining lots.

Questions of relatedness are central to our thinking about the next two starter home* sites – with two adjacent lots, an obvious coalition is established from the outset. Moreover, the idea of familial similarity and divergence relative to 3106 and the experiments that generated the pilot project's character frame the next challenge in the starter home* investigation – pushing a newly established logic to adapt, evolve, and generate progressive, ambitious, imaginative responses in the starter home typology.

1.

2.

3.

References & Works consulted

Adler, Margot. "Behind the Ever-Expanding American Dream House." National Public Radio, July 4, 2006, sec. All Things Considered.

Albrecht, Donald. World War II and the American Dream: How Wartime Building Changed a Nation. MIT Press, 1994.

Altman, Karen E. "Consuming Ideology: The Better Homes in America Campaign." Critical Studies in Mass Communication 7 (1990): 286–307.

American Planning Association. Modernizing State Planning Statutes. The Growing Smart Working Papers 462/463, 1996.

"Architects' Small House Service Bureau ASHSB Records," n.d. Minnesota Historical Society.

Arnold, Chris. "Sluggish Housing Market a Product of Millions of 'Missing Households.'" National Public Radio, June 18, 2014.

Belsky, Eric S., Christopher E. Herbert, and Jennifer H. Molinsky. Homeownership Built to Last: Balancing Access, Affordability, and Risk after the Housing Crisis. Washington, D.C.: The Brookings Institution, 2014.

Belsky, Eric S, Michael Schill, and Anthony Yezer. "The Effect of the Community Reinvestment Act on Bank and Thrift Home Purchase Mortgage Lending." Joint Center for Housing Studies:

Harvard University, August 2001.

Benjamin, Richard. The Money Pit, 1986.

Bennett, Donna S. "Condominium Homeownership in the United States: A Selected Annotated Bibliography of Legal Sources." Law Library Journal 103, no. 2 (n.d.): 2011–16.

Boustan, Leah P., and Robert A. Margo. "A Silver Lining to White Flight? White Suburbanization and African-American Homeownership, 1940-1980." Journal of Urban Economics 78 (2013): 71–80.

Bowman, Ann, and Michael A. Pagano. Terra Incognita: Vacant Land and Urban Strategies. Georgetown University Press, 2010.

———. "Vacant Land in Cities: An Urban Resource." The Brookings Institution, n.d.

Callis, Robert R, and Melissa Kresin. "Residential Vacancies and Homeownership in the First Quarter 2014." U.S. Dept. of Commerce: Social, Economic, and Housing Statistics Division, April 2014.

Center for Transit-Oriented Development, and Center for Neighborhood Technology. "The Affordability Index: A New Tool for Measuring the True Affordability of a Housing Choice." The Brookings Institution Metropolitan Policy Program Urban Markets Initiative, n.d.

Colton, Kent W. Housing in the Twenty-First

Century: Achieving Common Ground. Wertheim Publications in Industrial Relations. Harvard University Press, 2003.

Dietz, Robert, and Natalia Siniavskaia. "The Geography of Home Size and Occupancy." National Association of Home Builders, n.d.

Easterling, Keller. Organization Space: Landscapes, Highways, and Houses in America. MIT Press, 2001.

Ehrenhalt, Alan. The Great Inversion and the Future of the American City. New York: Random House, 2013.

Emrath, Paul. "Characteristics of Homes Started in 2012: Size Increase Continues." National Association of Home Builders, 2013.

Fischel, William A. "An Economic History of Zoning and a Cure for Its Exclusionary Effects." Dartmouth College, December 2001.

Frederick, Christine. Selling Mrs. Consumer, n.d.

Glaeser, Edward L. "Rethinking the Federal Bias Toward Homeownership." Cityscape: A Journal of Policy Development and Research 13, no. 2 (2011): 5–37.

Grebler, Leo, David M. Blank, and Louis Winnick. Capital Formation in Residential Real Estate: Trends and Prospects. Princeton University Press, 1956.

Hartman, Chester, and Robin Drayer. "Military-Family Housing: The Other Public-Housing Program." Housing and Society 17, no. 3 (1990).

Hillier, Amy E. "Who Received Loans? Home Owners' Loan Corporation Lending and Discrimination in Philadelphia in the 1930's." Journal of Planning History 2, no. 1 (2003): 3–24.

Hodgins, Eric. Mr. Blandings Builds His Dream House, 1946.

Joint Center for Housing Studies: Harvard University. "The State of the Nation's Housing: Housing Challenges," 2014.

Keller Easterling GSAPP. Call It Home: The House That Private Enterprise Built, n.d.

Kolko, Jed. "Why the Homeownership Rate Is Misleading." The New York Times, January 30, 2014.

Leichenko, Robin M. "Growth and Change in U.S. Cities and Suburbs." Growth and Change 32 (Summer 2001): 326–54.

"Median and Average Square Feet of Floor Area in New Single-Family Houses Completed by Location: 1973-2010." Census Bureau, n.d.

Metropolitan Policy Program. "State of Metropolitan America: On the Front Lines of Demographic Transformation." Brookings Institute, 2010.

Miller, Joshua J. "Snapshot of Home Ownership in Local Housing Markets." National Association of Home Builders, March 2014.

Piazzesi, Monika, Martin Schneider, and Selale Tuzel. "Housing, Consumption, and Asset Pricing." Journal of Financial Economics 83 (2007): 531–69.

Potter, H.C. Mr. Blandings Builds His Dream House, 1948.

Rosler, Martha. Semiotics of the Kitchen, 1975.

Sarkar, Mousumi. "Home American Homes Vary By the Year They Were Built." United States Census Bureau, June 2011.

Schwartz, Alex F. Housing Policy in the United States: An Introduction. New York: Routledge, 2006.

Shanken, Andrew M. 194X: Architecture, Planning, and Consumer Culture on the American Home Front. Minneapolis: University of Minnesota Press, 2009.

Shiller, Robert J. "Why Home Prices Change (or Don't)." The New York Times, April 13, 2013.

Taylor, Heather. "Cost of Constructing a Home." National Association of Home Builders, January 2014.

Twiss, Pamela, and James A. Martin. "Conventional and Military Public Housing for Families." Social Service Review 73, no. 2 (1999): 240-60.

US Census Bureau. "Housing Characteristics: 2010." U.S. Dept. of Commerce: Economics and Statistics Administration, October 2011.

———. "Measuring America: The Decennial Censuses From 1790 to 2000." U.S. Dept. of Commerce: Economics and Statistics Administration, September 2002.

U.S. Department of Housing and Urban Development. "2013 Characteristics of New Housing." U.S. Dept. of Commerce: Economics and Statistics Administration, n.d.

Weiss, Marc A. The Rise of the Community Builders: The American Real Estate Industry and Urban Land Planning. Beard Books, 2002.

What Works Collaborative. "Rental Market Stresses: Impacts of the Great Recession on Affordability and Multifamily Lending." Joint Center for Housing Studies: Harvard University, July 2011.

Woodstock Institute. "A Lifetime of Assets: Asset Preservation, Trends and Interventions in Asset Stripping Services and Products." National Community Reinvestment Coalition, n.d.

Wright, Gwendolyn. Building the Dream: A Social History of Housing in America. Cambridge: MIT Press, 1983.

Zhou, Yu, and Donald R. Haurin. "On the Determinants of House Value Volatility." JRER 32, no. 4 (2010).

James Casabere's "Landscape with Houses", 2011

Made in the USA
Middletown, DE
03 June 2023